Signaletics

AKRON SERIES IN POETRY

AKRON SERIES IN POETRY
Mary Biddinger, Editor

Emilia Phillips, *Signaletics*
Seth Abramson, *Thievery*
Steve Kistulentz, *Little Black Daydream*
Jason Bredle, *Carnival*
Emily Rosko, *Prop Rockery*
Alison Pelegrin, *Hurricane Party*
Matthew Guenette, *American Busboy*
Joshua Harmon, *Le Spleen de Poughkeepsie*
David Dodd Lee, *Orphan, Indiana*
Sarah Perrier, *Nothing Fatal*
Oliver de la Paz, *Requiem for the Orchard*
Rachel Dilworth, *The Wild Rose Asylum*
John Minczeski, *A Letter to Serafin*
John Gallaher, *Map of the Folded World*
Heather Derr-Smith, *The Bride Minaret*
William Greenway, *Everywhere at Once*
Brian Brodeur, *Other Latitudes*
Jeff Gundy, *Spoken among the Trees*
Alison Pelegrin, *Big Muddy River of Stars*
Roger Mitchell, *Half/Mask*
Ashley Capps, *Mistaking the Sea for Green Fields*
Beckian Fritz Goldberg, *The Book of Accident*
Clare Rossini, *Lingo*
Vern Rutsala, *How We Spent Our Time*
Kurt Brown, Meg Kearney, Donna Reis, Estha Weiner, eds.,
    Blues for Bill: A Tribute to William Matthews
Sharmila Voorakkara, *Fire Wheel*
Dennis Hinrichsen, *Cage of Water*
Lynn Powell, *The Zones of Paradise*

Titles published since 2003.
For a complete listing of titles published in the
series, go to www.uakron.edu/uapress/poetry

Signaletics

Emilia Phillips

The University of Akron Press
Akron, Ohio

17   16   15   14   13   5   4   3   2   1

ISBN: 978-1-937378-54-7 (cloth)
ISBN: 978-1-937378-55-4 (paper)
ISBN: 978-1-937378-56-1 (ePub)
ISBN: 978-1-937378-57-8 (ePDF)

LIBRARY OF CONGRESS CATALOGING-IN-PUBLICATION DATA
Phillips, Emilia.
  Signaletics / Emilia Phillips. – First edition.
      p. cm. — (Akron series in poetry)
  ISBN 978-1-937378-55-4 (pbk. : alk. paper) — ISBN 978-1-937378-54-7 (cloth : alk. paper)
  I. Title.
  PS3616.H4553S56 2013
  811'.6–dc23
                          2013014443

∞ The paper used in this publication meets the minimum requirements of ANSI / NISO Z39.48–1992 (Permanence of Paper).

Cover: Mug shot of Thomas Bede, photographer unknown, 22 November 1928, Central Police Station, Sydney. NSW Police Forensic Photography Archive, Justice & Police Museum, Historic Houses Trust of NSW, Sydney, Australia. Used with permission.

Signaletics was designed and typeset in Baskerville by Amy Freels and printed on sixty-pound natural and bound by Bookmasters of Ashland, Ohio.

Contents

IV

for Jeremy & in memory of Nick

"the recidivist, without daring to contest his present personality, denies his past identity, and repudiates the previous arrests and sentences which are attributed to him, seeking to put them on the back of a brother or cousin who has disappeared, or else of some unknown person resembling him exactly."
—Alphonse Bertillon, *Signaletic Instructions including the theory and practice of Anthropometrical Identification*

"when you placed one of these incomprehensible, monstrous objects so that it was reflected in the incomprehensible, monstrous mirror, a marvelous thing happened; minus by minus equaled plus, everything was restored, everything was fine, and the shapeless speckledness became in the mirror a wonderful, sensible image; flowers, a ship, a person, a landscape."
—Nabokov, *Invitation to a Beheading*

Subject in the Position of the Soldier with No Arms

Fill out your frame. Balancing is an act of forgetting.
Here are stones for your pocket and lead for the toe

of your shoe. Here, for an ear, a halved shell
and calf leather for a stopgap tongue. My father kept

the jar that rattled with the slug tweezed from his thigh—
metal on the X-ray like blood inside a mosquito

locked in cretaceous amber. Here's the missing finger
of the porcelain Christ—delicate as an eyelash, a blue

flake of paint from his robe. Don't ask where the teeth are
you exchanged for coins as a child. Your first lesson

in compromise. And what was next—Discipline?
Duty? In the mouth of my mother, a molar dissolves

like soap. Here's a shackle for your ankle, a pin to hold
your elbow together, three screws for a broken heel.

You must hold still. There's a storm in the western sky.
Beneath god's empty shoulder socket, you're a hailstone

of nerves, the fist clenched at the end of a phantom arm.

I

Teratoma

a benign tumor that often develops other recognizable
features of the body

A lump above her hipbone M. had me
       touch in the girls' bathroom as she lifted
              her uniform Oxford, size of an unripe

peach, as hard, she mistook for a knot
       from a volleyball fall. The doctors gave her
              the jar to hold when she came out from under—

three teeth, fully formed, a tuft of black hair,
       a lung, peanut-sized, that trembled like a yolk
              when she raised it to look. No one was to know.

Her desk empty for a week. We began each Bible class
       with a prayer & nominated our requests
              as if for awards. I was silent. She was gone

so we prayed for her. We prayed for all
       the absent—the girl who went missing
              for a month at the end, near graduation.

The word was mono. But once we ripped into
       summer, we saw her out with the baby & he was
              beautiful, as secrets go. *Touch here,*

my friend told me. *Be easy.* Over her right kidney
       the teratoma hovered. She cried when I pressed
              it with my thumb. I made my first boyfriend

fuck me through silk panties as if this would keep
        me pure. But then I didn't care about being pure. I wanted to be
                nothing, to come out

of my uniform, hipbones shrugging off
        the grey skirt, I wanted to rise through the collar
                like blue flame from a Bunsen burner,

leave so that no one knew, my clothes holding
        the shape I gave them in the desk. *They'll fall*
                off, she said, when I looped my fingers

with rubber bands until blood starved, white—
        I was a stranger to myself. My one Hindu friend shoved
                her books to the floor when our world

religion teacher said her many gods with their many arms
        would dissolve like salt. Here, we lifted one another, our voices
                scalpel-edged. We began with a prayer, & there we ended it.

Vanitas (Latent Print)

The nurse's ink would not do: so heavy it flooded
the ridges to smudge the white paper my father
pressed each of my brother's fingers to. A record

wanted, the made engraving like shoe-tread on the steely
moon & into a pendant for his wife, N.'s mother—
this, the last dotage, son to father. How impossible

creation was then, watching from my corner, as he bent
over the bed, my child-sibling paling in
lips & cheeks & hollowed chest, & darkening finally

across his backside, crown of his head, as the veins fractaled
indigo toward the empty ears. *How long will you break me
in pieces with words?* When my father, shaking & saying

over & over, *This will not work—it's too heavy,* & wept again
as the ink wept from the sponge, the nurse at my request
brought an aluminum can to which we pressed the hands

for prints my father, unfathered, would lift later with dust.

Entra Tutto

"Why, man, he doth bestride the narrow world
Like a Colossus..."
—Cassius, Julius Caesar

At the opening ceremony of the battle reenactment, the Vice President was to speak on History—his ancestor's role in the war—but not those slight skeletons or their winking lines of succession inhumed like feral kings in the dusky peat of ordinary memory.

•

For days, truckfuls of men with medias-bellum beards set up canvas tents along the creek, rattling their reproduction hardtack tins, as over their newspaper and starter log campfires they sing, *in forma paupris to God,* *"Lay bare thine arm, stretch forth thy rod..."*

They are, like the infantry they approximate, trespassing.

•

(dispatch from Capt. Sam Fletcher Cheney:)

We began to feel as if we should return...

•

I woke that morning to soundlessness, no *thrr-thrr* of traffic over Reed's Bridge, J. already to work, and the throughroad closed. At either end, police barricades. Soon, a patrolman came to the house and said, *You can leave today but you can't get back in.*

•

In Cesare Lombroso's *Criminal Man*, the torso of his proto-reprobate is crowded with tattoos. On his penis, we read: ENTRA TUTTO. *It all goes in.*

•

I cannot remember if the stump I teetered on, alone, with a handwritten sign had ever been a tree while we lived there, for memory and landscape are so similar in their attritions, but there, before me, a tree's shadow, yes, slack as a dead man's hand, while I became the tree, studying the others that broke the pasture, how each touched another like one might a deaf person, lightly but with intention so as not to alarm, startle, but with the trees I had never been so gentle, once digging a bowie into the bark and retrieving a Minié ball, acorn-sized, swirled with lead tarnish, a dark little world cloudy with moods.

•

(dispatch:)

> *The messenger brought the wrong message. Longstreet exploded the line.*
> *We rode to Chattanooga without stopping or looking behind.*

•

Did we have ghosts? An infestation, like squirrels in the attic, rodents in the walls? Often I walked along the split-beam fence, white as lime, at night and saw movement in the overgrown field behind us—deer or the heifer Mr. X owned, chewing to oblivion with her cud.

Teenage boys gathered under the bridge with *The Book of the Dead* and encircled themselves with their mothers' table salt. We found cats, their eyes blistered, strung up by their haunches, and once, a rat terrier gutted on a boulder as if a rabbit butchered for stew.

Spiders clung, dull starbursts to their silken constellations in the garage, and a field mouse I found on the center rack of my oven, dead, its white tail drooped to touch the coils.

•

(eclogue:)

—Did we have spirits?

they had to move ahead by moving backward

•

The characters of the Danse Macabre at the Church of the Holy Trinity in Hrastovlje do not dance, instead they march toward an enthroned skeleton: first the pope, the royal couple, a cardinal, bishop, monk and burgher, the merchant, an ordinary man, the cripple, and a child who leaps from his cradle to join the procession.

•

A friend's mother with whom I carpooled kept us out of school to see the next president speak at the regional airport. When I touched the sleeve of his navy sport coat as he moved through the crowd, his face obliterated in sunlight, he withdrew his hand and pushed on.

•

On the corkboard are two postcards from my father: *Salam from Iraq* and *Greetings from Ancient Mesopotamia.* He wrote on the back of one: *A view from where I am in the world.*

•

(dispatch:)

We arrived in camp. Beautiful here. Scouts are leaving now.

•

I waited but no one passed. No motorcade. Only the distant rumblings of false cannon fire, the cracks of rifles. I walked the middle of the empty road, sign at my side, to the Park and stood at the entrance where the trees arched and clawed one another to canopy the road.

I did not go any further. But it was all there, somehow, in the distance through the thicket in spits of fire and the fallen. I could see it—like staring at an image and looking away to find it followed your gaze, only now, ephemeral and light, as if woven from golden hair.

Latent Print

Besmearing upon the plate, gelatin
cooked to harden with chrome alum,
cooled & then the layer of emulsion

poured center & tilted to cover
the surface entire. For two days,
Eakins frames the plates. The model

by the window fingers the sash
of her robe. Unnamed
in the photo, she sprawls, deadweight

in his arms, nude, hard shadows
beveling her curves. She appears helpless with
her fallen head, neck

exposed. *If you're ever kidnapped, bite
the car door*, my father said one Sunday
after the divorce, Crown Vic en route

to his office. Teeth marks. *I can find you
that way.* Inside he sat me down & held
each of my fingers to an ink

pad, smothering ridges in black,
& then from left to right, prints
he rolled on a white card. *These are yours—*

they don't change. In his portrait
carrying a woman, Eakins too is naked,
shoulders slung back. Behind him

an empty chair, three easels. Shuttered
by a student, the camera sears image
on dry plate. As I

stare the woman grows heavier
& heavier in his arms. A lover maybe,
paid girl. Never let go, he will never.

I will find you. My father points to
the scans on the IBM*: Whorl loop
whorl   whorl   whorl*

Triptych: Automata

*"The laws of nature still rule them, very little corrupted by ours;
and they are in such a state of purity that I am sometimes vexed
that they were unknown earlier..."*
—*Michel de Montaigne, "Of Cannibals"*

I. "Francine," after his deceased daughter

—René Descartes, 1649

Uncarved, the fingers. Their delineation
in simple brushstrokes, black.

                         Her mouth
open. Francine, her name—*Daughter*. From creation
always the chagrin of imperfection—

effigy's insensate rigor. Descartes, traveling
for the last time to Sweden, lugs the heavy box
aboard.
           Inside the girl sleeps but cannot

sleep, as the dead do. His lungs will bellow
& collapse. The ship rocks. Ball in socket,

the head swivels. Endemic or given, the mind
winds down, clockwork ticking.

II. "Tipu's Tiger"

—French craftsmen for Tipu, Sultan of Mysore, 1790

From the bodywork: an organ roar
forged by wind funnels & bellows in the belly

of the tiger vised at the throat of the British soldier, rubicund
faced & red coated, when the crank is turned

again & again by the French artisan, & the sultan,
hysterical with laughter, desires the whole East Indian

Company prostrate, turning from the jaws, arm falling
& lifting, falling again, while the mouth remains

unable to open & the wooden skull, entirely
hollow, rattles with the creature's thunder.

III. "The Flute Player"

—*Jacques de Vaucauson, 1738*

Twelve songs to prove faculty, nine
    bellows to forge & three pipes
        to transmit wind to the oral cavity

where a thin tongue controls
    release across the riser, activating
        the shaft with vibration while the fingers,

padded leather, piston their combinations
    on the keys—the rhythm, perfunctory—
        & the notes unwavering in intonation

remain untainted by innervation,
    even as the lips, rigid & wooden,
        narrow toward a higher pitch.

Bertillonage Fragment, I:
Taille

The tongues
of some

are broad leather
whips

no real

muscle just hide
& oil & sting

no defense

they revise their bodies
by breaking

bones to scars

they kiss
their pride

some punks
are larger than they

seem laughing

bending
iron

with pissed-on bed sheets

we may measure
by their size

their eyes

widen their fingers
fill with blood

no bricks
or chains can hold

these hoods or cells
or sentence

upward
these men

rise & like lightning
expire

Blues Dream

The shadow doe stepping into the highway's
        calm wakes me from diaphanous sleep
                in the passenger's seat, from the dream

in which I ask you to walk with me—
        sandals ignited, our garments inflamed.
                Though when we are naked, we are unscathed,

bodies daubed in ash. All the windows
        open. Unbalanced, the tires slow in their rhythm
                warping as the radio creaks in and out

of a Dandridge station. We stop. The deer
        ahead, posed. Our flashing headlights
                goad her out of a trance and onward—

hooving into the fast lane just as the wind
        wake of a passing car rocks our small vessel.
                Beginning in one dark field, the end

is in another. How could I go without you?
        This time last year, blocks in view of the Potomac,
                we walked in freezing rain: my dress,

your pant legs, siphon water from the street
        slicked with oil and light, as if we were drawing
                versicolor neon or *ignus fatuus*

onto us and in before we entered
        the concert hall shaking our umbrella,
                footprints wet and tickets offered

to the usher. *G14 for the missus.*
        G13, sir. Down the dark aisle
                to our seats, we were guided, shaking—

indistinguishable among the shadow
        crowd by Frisell who shades his eyes against
                the stage lights before beginning the endless

set with "Blues Dream" spoken not in the pure
        language of blues but rather its pidgin,
                chimera of catatonia, repine, stealth—

his face contorting, mouth agape, fingers drossed
        in the strings' tarnish as he avulses
                a note from the Telecaster like a sore tooth

from a black gum. You disappear in the dark
        beside me. Always. Pulling alongside the deer's
                body—the other car, gone—one sinew

thick as a bass string in her neck
        quivered. Nearly dawn. We were so far
                from home yet near

another with all the windows open
        and the deer dying—the cold and wavering I
                who roves in darkness, waking to a great light.

II

Diaspora

When the world goes pearly

in the helio range with ash and element,
and whatever was

understood in corpus
is suddenly forgotten—

like the reason why I walked

into this room—

when there is no one,
there will be a few,

perhaps, in a sleepy

orbit. And when they finally lose
communication, one will ask

nothing, over and over,

Do you read? — *Do you read?*

Except this will not be

the language he speaks in,
though the language will be the same
as it was before.

One will cry. Another, laugh

and slam his brow

against the indestructible
window until he's bleeding,

forehead split like the mango

he once shook from a tree,
until the sound that lives on

between the panes

becomes him, becomes the elegant
slander of his life he hears

or thinks

he hears, eavesdropping,
in this way, on the future.

●

If one of you can
point to this and say,

This is untrue,

then it is.

When and *If* are old friends
who write

but never visit, a withdrawal
of the senses

from a violent land.

I can't remember
why I am

standing on this threshold,

every *thing* before me

a cloud

beginning to scatter,
while gravity

looks through me,

down my body
and into my shoes.

Cross Section

Into the bath drawn cold for fever
I lower until the water covers all
but breasts, eyes, & nose—

One o'clock & B.'s body
is now in the chamber where a magnet

will skim her ashes for screws, bone
fasteners, & crowns. The boy
behind me on the plane asked why

I was wearing the blue mask
& held a cup of ice to my neck

& wrists. *Pressure points,* I told him but didn't
explain. At security
my bags & body probed. *Why*

are you traveling? Why are you flushed?
A pacemaker explodes in the fired

chamber, but the heart slows
in cold water, the fever drawn
from the body: hot to cold,

hot to cold. In the terminal waiting
for the next flight out,

I studied the magazine
cross section of Al-Jazari's elephant
clepsydra in whose hollow

body a bowl continually fills, becoming heavy
with each hour.

The Study Heads

—after Franz Messerschmidt's Character Heads

Parts of us we don't precisely feel until in pain.

For this, we are surface creatures, capable of expression
and loss. Think of *magnetism*, Mesmer's

panacea, his patients going willful, each into a noose
roped to a baquet tub of alloyed copper—

in want of power or forgiveness, *repair*. But what comes?

Only the grimace, hysterical laugh, or monolith

stare. But if their facial exaggerations, cast in medias res
by Franz Messerschmidt, caused the body to react,

tense, with a tingling in the cheek, a light head, a mind to work
over the corporeal field, fallowed by a latent

decision to possess some trifle
of vigor, is this not a minor resurrection?

By proxy, even?

. . .

The evening after we saw
the heads in circular congress

at the Belvedere, an American   (I could *tell*—
by his suit and walk to the table) shifted

in his seat beside us when J. asked me where
my father was now.
                                        —*Back in Bagram.*

Perhaps it was the attraction of an idea and not strictly empirical
magnetism, the body as a somatic

conduit, completed

by a lacquer of ions, that Mesmer was after.

From him, we've earned the word *mesmerize.*

The man was listening, leaning in, ever so
slightly, and when I turned in

to his gaze, he spread

his white napkin across his lap, studying it—
as if it was a redacted map that waited

to be redrawn, *resurrected,*

which is, after all, the byword of memory,
collective and, therefore, impure—

And after a sip of his sparkling water,
his hands, in afterthought

or mindlessness
like a mother to her child's hair,

smoothed the creases down.

. . .

From Arabic, we digested *zenith*,

albatross, and *ghoul*.
                          Messerschmidt so angered the spirit
of classical proportion with the contorted

faces, he claimed he was tortured

nightly for transgressions

against "*high* art." He began self-portraits

in the mirror, pinching the loose loom

of skin above a rib, *twisted*—.

And if he was both the spirit and himself,
then so be it. It changes nothing.

Guilt is as symmetrical,

and classical, as a wingspan, a stable

molecule, *zero* . . .

...

...*decipher*... *arsenal*...

crimson...   *gauze*...   *algorithm*...   *assassin*...

magazine...
            lacquer...   *jar*...

. . .

Weeks after,

I held the plastic medical container metered

for liquid though it rattled with the flattened
bullet that, from impact, looked like a crude watch

battery. My father, on leave, took his dog out

and came back with a tail-tucked mutt into
the kitchen, a gunshot wound in his thigh. Falling

to the floor, he ripped his t-shirt in front

of my grandmother to tourniquet—
The blood was fathomless, the femoral grazed....

On the phone, I misunderstood, heard:

ephemeral artery. You see, he thought someone was
trailing him, and maybe they *were*, but when

he drew his gun on a scattering of birds or a forsythia

that rustled at a neighbor's window, he was *sure*—
but the dog spooked and pulled the leash wrapped

around his wrist, lowering his gun in governance

of the trigger. And if, now, I think of Job,
saying, *I have said to corruption, Thou* art *my father,*

where now is my hope?

At the mirror, the torture of Messerschmidt was not his pain.

Waking this morning, I could not move,
the paralysis temporary—

mind awake, body endured—but no less

complete. As if a sarsen, sashed to
my waist, pulled me into gravity.

In the *Physiologus*,

Anonymous writes that when a lioness
gives birth to her whelp, she brings it forth

dead, and for three days, she minds it,
unsleeping,

pacing in dimly orchestrated paths, her body weeping
afterbirth,

until the sire—*God*, in the morality
of Anonymous,

though here, he's known as Consequence—
arrives, awakening the stillborn with his breath.

Of all the things I don't believe, I believe this the most.

As we walked the circle of heads, the sun resurrected
after days of rain. This was not the divine,

it was *the dramatic.*

Which is the byword of the sublime,
the prologue to death.

Shall I go the way whence I shall not return?

To its hard and bitter root,
my father knew the etymology of pain

I waited and listened this morning at the window
words collect. The torture

of Messerschmidt was to keep his eyes
open, though

the eyes, they always close.

Bertillonage Fragment, II:
Buste

Not heads or genitalia, legs
    or hands, but more torsos
        survive from classical architecture—
            so much defending
                a territory & drawing the opposite
                    sex in the lek arena depends on
                        chest puffing, the appearance of being
larger than
    the self; some men
        breathe in to fool the measurements,
            mistaking hollowness
                for girth: they are one, the statues
                of sturdy marble, solid muscle
                    of stone & permanent grace
even
    in pieces: abdomen joining
        back, buttocks, & pectoralis with organs
            & with heart, achene
                uncarved, the dormant
                germ inside.

Sublimation

I. Miscarriage

—after "The Turba Philosophorum"

My curio, my heart-murmur, the retching echoes
inside the shower babel: *red by the body* mixed

with it. Tenuous nature in the belly hidden
by the most subtle regimen, *wholly quicksilver.*

The mattress on the floor is darkened to infusion;
the pants, the panties froth in the sink, peroxide's

minor alchemy: I dreamed (*the fire and the vessel
sealed lest the body*) of the fox and her three

kits we saw in the cemetery, emerging from the den's
loggia of snow. The house holds the cold like marrow.

So the thief. I have made something from nothing,
and nothing again (*in all things, fire is that which eats*).

II. Prayer

If the madwoman I've become
              loves you beyond
love, inhumanly
                  human, borne
out of the Adoration
       of my own spirit, know

that prayer, too, is simply a process
       of the body
               toward one

of its two ends: regrowth
  (*and/or*)
           elimination.

III. Sleep

How to locate in the night, with a gasp, the footholds
    of consciousness while stupefied by sleep paralysis—

a car backfires (*a shot?*) as the inherited sidearm
    in the drawer weeps tarnish and the blue luciferin

of the squad car seizures the window on approach.
    You once thought an earthquake the neighbors making

love upstairs, but the berth of the tremor was in the heart's
    ballot box, the precincts of night. Somewhere, someone

else between Wake/Submerge. In the morning, you ask:
    Who sipped from this cup? (With a mauve scallop

of lipstick) —Or, *held this spoon?* (Crinolined with cross-
    stamped fingerprints) In this way, days spill from you. (White

sugar from a crooked spoon) There can be no emptiness
    without a vessel. Awake (*Are* you*?*) unable to move

and yet, asleep, without knowing, you rise and walk
    the empty hall, head bored through (*opened?*) by pupils.

IV. Marriage

(a paradox)

HE TOOK A WIFE HE WAS IN THE HABIT OF TAKING

V. War

The Harlan's Hawk circled the pond: sleek satellite of its own
hunger, above the egg hens pecking at algae drifts that settled
and sludged the basin in drought. It taloned off one and then another,
another. And so opened a door to death at the end of the corridor
of your life that you, for the first time, realized you walk toward:
now, crossing the yard with your grandmother's pocketbook
revolver in hand, a Bowie through a belt loop. And after you
severed the claw and tied a strip of your red t-shirt to the ankle,

Boy soldier, in the knife-size slice of sky, you saw the world
to come, hardened in reflection, made meaningful in its descent.

VI. Oeuvre

—after Ossian

[Shade-hand on throat.]

I look on thy war, my son;
I look, a dim meteor, from my cloud.

Goodnight,

— [familiar].

\- — \- — \- \-

dis   dah   dis   dah   dis dis

Ghost Sonnet

Ask the water to know my ankles,
and I ask for the flood.
                    Ask for the bridge—
it's the other side I want.
                    I see water

from everywhere but the bottom,
dark holes where boys dive and reach

into time, the scalloped mail of scales
peeling open a wrist....
                    Ask for the hand?
You ask for nails.
Ask for the bird of peace—
                    it's the crow,

driving the singing flocks
from suspension cables,
while a man passes me (we are strangers)
on a bicycle,
                    asking each
wooden plank we cross
                    to be one road.

III

In vacuo, Universal Studios

We begin in line. We end there.

In the gentle shuffle forward

of our incumbent spell.

We find the school of attention

in the school of boredom,

the *danse ennui* in the study

of shoes. In the queue,

time moves through a half-solid.

Air is just a fraction

away from liquid. We're all drowning,

slowly. Especially

in Florida. In my father's temple,

in the heat, a vein is swollen—

Lethe in my flower . . . In the fadeless garden . . .

If we could look inside the living

mind, I imagine, versions

of ourselves, miniscule and impure,

in a gridlock on the interstate.

This we call memory—

and then forget.

Each time we open the mind,

it dies like a movie

astronaut in a holey spacesuit.

Here, we measure time

in bodies. My father sweats

through his clothes.

I lean into the metal

railing, and the heat it holds

enters into me

like information.

Burning. Body after body,

we could keep on going—

beyond this moment we've existed in

here, past the line

and my father's old silence,

arriving at his new:

the sequence

of personless photos, mountains

in a war-country he sends

without caption. From these, I get:

"Love exists at terminus;

meaning, *in vacuo.*"

The Speech of Monkeys

*In 1893, R. L. Garner locked himself inside a cage in the
French Congo for three months to record and study the vocal
communication of primates.*

Garner's winding of the arm
and the needle's scratch on the plate of tin
recorded the female Capuchin

chattering in her cage. Her mate, black-bagged
by the zookeeper, & taken away
   thrashing—
               This is the recording—

the words shiver
in & out of you,   tuning

fork cast in mania's pitch. Unplugging
all the electronics, you noosed

the lamps with their cords & drove a screw-
driver into the cell repeating, *I'm sorry.*

*Your call cannot be completed
as dialed.* The phonograph called
the male Capuchin in the voice of his mate—

over & over   the tin plate spinning
the same chattering. Into the black
throat of the phonograph,
          all the way in,

he reached, grasping nothing.
This is this is
the recording. Untranslatable,

the argot throws itself at the bars
of the ear. To thin voices,

we wither, thin hands.
Frequency vacillating
in a molar's filling, your wife's underwire extracted
with pliers. The television's skull

lifted above your head & thrown
onto the rocks below the deck,

its one snowy eye blinded

to your image, & the speakers'
honeycomb mouth, fractured to silence.
& here where the distance is cogged
with houses, unending, the gears' teeth sink in—
toward the self-

locked cage where you wait, the shadows approach
from the jungle, quiet
& rising from their knuckles.

Post

From London with 103° fever to my father, APO HE 09342

The Kurdistan honey you sent
I drizzled in warm sour mash

where it suspended mid-glass in viscous

curls. *A girl from Tennessee drinks Tennessee*
whiskey, joked the barman, unfolding
a napkin before me.
                            Do you like your country

music, too? Fever, self-medication: four shots
& then sprawling in my hotel bed, watching
crime shows, Scotland Yard murder while dozing

in & out of a hive of dreams: the fire like honey
clinging. *Nothing burns that way,* you say.
It overruns everything. Pneumonia—

                    Why didn't I go sooner?

The doctor muses: *Your American insurance*
I'm obliged to trouble with? I take the pills,

swallow them whole (*pink bullets*).
You hear explosions as far away it seems as stars

& as bantam. You're asked to know a people

by their fingerprints & therefore, what it's taken
& given. In the lab, the A/C smells sweet,
the coolant resists dissolution, dripping...

The boom & sibilance of the old year
on Trafalgar recedes on the TV

into the dream of you as the faceless keeper

approaching with fire, the smoke to lull
the bees that fall
                    soundlessly, having eaten

from all fruits, following the design.

The Ear: General Form &
Separation of the Internal Windings

Even in the lock a spring is quivering
a note   stunned by the unfit precision
of my mother's bobby pin

                      & it must be
my mother's for she's what's held
& kept in its place
& what isn't   (How many times she's left
the doors unlocked when she was home...)
She breaks
the pin in the lock—   She's lost
her keys again   & the color on her lips...

Once a man came at sunrise into the kitchen
    asking
for a cup of coffee with cream
& extra sugar   She heaved the cast iron
skillet over her head   & the man's
nose like a walnut cracked—

                        congealed grease
wobbled & slid from the pan & smacked
the linoleum
        & my legs

I was young
a baby   My mother stayed
up the whole night...

                      listening
to the police   radio
            to my father.
   This is Badge 490...

the hot pursuits he was in

The dispatcher
told my mother to get off the air
when she called   *Kenny, come home.*

•

The morning after my mother breaks into her own
home   two joggers find a hen

impaled
on the wrought-iron fence of the cemetery
where her family is   buried

dried blood
at the hen's throat a fruit knife opened   to silence
its terror   like rust eating

a hole

Day Is Done.

It's nothing

my husband says when I wake him thinking   I hear
the floors creak downstairs,
or a flowerpot broken for the hidden key.

•

They were all black
the old police geldings
on the farm my father used
to look after
whenever the owner
took his wife
on trips to unswimmable waters
cold & turbidly beautiful.

I stood on a pine stump
a horse named Robert chewed
& held the salt
lick for him as long
as his tongue would slug
its length. One day
a white truck with silver trailer
arrived while my father
was off at the feed store
& its driver said he had to take
the horses to town
for a funeral.

I watched from the stump
as the man led one
by one the six geldings
muzzled grey
up the ramp & into the trailer.
I watched too
as he shut the gate,
& watched the truck stall
before it hawed away.

•

                    She has to crawl
in through the window when the lock jams
& her purse doesn't jingle

                            with keys settled

in the bottom   She takes off her navy pumps
& lets them fall
A porch nail catches

                        her hose
as she lifts her leg   knee
to the ledge Her hose snaps back

now   limp as a half-sloughed
snakeskin

            How could I know this?

My mother—states
away   on her porch in an irreconcilable

                                    dark
the streetlights buzzed out & maybe…

no   there's rain   Ears & ears & ears
clot the catalogs of Bertillon—

                        owing to the many hollows
and ridges which furrow it   it's the most important

means of identification in the human visage

•

My father wants to buy me an instrument
just one but any one

I want   as long
as I promise to play for at least three years

I pick the trumpet because it looks the most
confident in its own sound   without
all the extra keys   & reeds

just one

mouthpiece to slide in   & I could imagine
my breath blowing through it   the paths
possible
                        I could see the pistons

shift the puzzle   change the tracks
I could taste

the metal of my own blood

•

There's nothing there,
my husband says
when I say voices
are wraithing in
through the amplifier
when he holds
the guitar

like that.

He shifts in his seat
& the voices

focus
into volume
tuning the strings
to a frequency
of a CB signal,
the local news,
or the stars—

Quiet, now.
I can almost hear
what they're saying . . .

•

Even the men in the saddles believe their ears
are gold
              as brittle & brilliant & malleable
They don't hear the guns anymore
burning through their powder
                         They wear their hearts
under Kevlar   & the dead

what do they do?
                What do they mean?
They're waiting under the window

flush against the wall
setting off silent alarms
                    as they leave
in rafts made of the light
bones of birds

       My mother in the morning after
wakes to her hand swollen
      She wraps herself in gauze

She's given up the name that is
my father's
      She says   *Good morning*

Who's there?

She hears whispers in her ear & the night's echoes
at the break of day folding their tents like gypsies
& as silently stealing away.

Bertillonage Fragment, III:
Longueur de la tête & Largeur de la tête

A bowl which we carry with no hands
A dark wine

of thought rippling with each step
Some men spill

Some overflow
The acts of men are difficult to understand

The bread entering us becoming body
in the mind

The wine the blood the deed
into guilt transfiguring

Other men have no faith
in the law

Some men act on passion
The larger the brain

the more intelligent the animal
Some need proof

of their humanity
through punishment

Latent Print: Interrogation Helix

Someone to call to ask questions. *No, Your Honor.* A reference for an increase in security clearance. *I did not touch the avulsed tooth; I only saw it in the gravel, blood-caked with dust.* Someone understood I was nervous. I was not nervous. *He swung and missed: self-defense.* My father taught me if someone grabbed my arm to turn toward the thumb and kick the scrotum. *He was the boyfriend of a girl I knew from class. I'd never met him before. He was belligerent. He wouldn't leave when we asked.* Someone wondered when I saw my father last. *She was already in the car. She didn't witness a damn thing.* Someone knew I must have missed him when he was gone. *I left because I hate violence, not because I was scared of him. We're getting married next June.* Someone was curious about my stance on the war. *I was right behind him. No, two blows. Not three.* Someone inquired if he ever mentioned anything about his work. *(laughs) He makes false teeth.* Someone knew I questioned him and what he was doing. *He could've saved it—if only he'd kept it in cold milk.*

Cuspis

To learn to make false teeth,
one must pull a blade
through a blue bar of soap,
carving to the size
of a bullet. Then, the fine
etching—the exact angle
of a lingual ridge, precise
contour of a right maxillary
cuspid's cingulum.

        Theorists
say that to know human anatomy
one must recreate it, little
by little: porcelain tooth,

                   glass
eye, artificial heart.

IV

Ars Poetica (Latent Print)

Back between seats, to floorboard
and fetal, to lie down in the open

city atlas, and begin to think of the self
as only those parts that break cover:

reflection, whimper. The blue light's
agyre, a voice almost singing her

dispatch: *Calling all officers*: Such is
the engine: such the work

that may be done with it, and there
in the back of my father's city-issue,

I became nothing as a child knows
nothing: absence from the knowledge

of others, beyond smallness, to stay low
as told, to do as the father says even

as he leaves, Beretta holstered, and after
a time, grow curious, to rise

from hiding to see a figure approaching
in the mirror: and then the mirror.

Latent Print: Indicia

[2] postcards enscrawled with *Salam from Iraq* and *Greetings from Ancient Mesopotamia*

[1] Bible bound in desert-camo leather, free from the Moral and Wellness Center

[3] Kuwaiti bills and a sack full of pre-invasion coins embossed with date palms

[1] *Coca-cola Light* can branded in Arabic, drammed, rinsed, and de-tabbed

[1] CD, Memorex, filled with pictures taken since arrival, most from a transport helicopter

USE ADDITIONAL SHEETS AS NECESSARY.

•

1.

Do not refer to each other
by first names or initials of first
names. Abbreviate

roles. Ex.: *D* for *Dad,*   *D* for *Daughter,*

and *B/ S* in relative correlation for *Brother/ Son.*

The only persons you'll need to know.

2.

       Never refer to the name
       of your hometown. Refer only to *home.*

3.

       If, periodically, the email address
       of the sender changes, know it's for his
       security and yours.

4.

       If there are long stretches
       of silence, do not assume circumstance. Wait
       until you are told.

Skin Mags

Technicoloresque to dinge, torn
                  creases, & bodies out of fashion—

girls vix from the racks of the vintage
                  bookstore under headlines of *Knight, Nugget,*

Gent, & *Genesis.* In a mildewed bill
                  with its rusty efflorescence of staples, the girls

remain unchanged by the nivation of desire:
                  erosion, meltwater, the giving up

& letting in, the gone & irrelevant, the mags
                  stuffed in floorboard, attic, basement,

a strongbox. Not even in the act
                  but the suggestion of it, the whole arc

of action lost. One redhead almost
                  there—*almost.* Oh, there's so much

she's done but never known, all a version
                  of what the viewer desires in anyone:

mate, potential energy: what comes
                  next, what came before, the half-second

of teetering preceding stability or
                    the fall with & from one's lover

however changed from the realms of light,
                    the gloss, clothed in brightness. All of them now

old enough to be my grandmother
                    if I imagine the girls as women, not image,

as persons. I try not to think
                    where their likenesses have been, which ones

dead & what it means for anyone,
                    including me, to desire an image of the body

ephemeral. We snare
                    our ghosts for historical consequence, nail

them to our heels so they fan & waver
                    like shadows behind us as we haunt our own

lives with flashlights, compulsions, spit,
                    or under the fluorescents where I turn the page,

envying the pleasure/pain constellation
                    of athanasia & unrelease, as it was with us

when we laid our words open, & now as I count the bills
                    & smile meekly at the cashier, I can imagine

only after—towel around her shivering
                    body, how alone the redhead must have

dressed before stepping through the steel
                    doors & into the afternoon light.

Niedecker's Iron

All night the shirts unbutton
from the hangers, drop

on their own to the floor. I gather
them in the morning.
                              A snakeskin
yesterday, on the water, gave me
a start—the eye scales, pearl. Slough.
Deflesh.
            Slaughter. Today, no word

from you, Louis, or your dear
Paul—
            just the hissing again
of the iron, the steam blinding
the window.

Reading Joyce on U.S. Flight 2309

         Forgive the body
its inordinance: sweat, flush, & death

grip. Or an instinct ad nauseum
of late: desire. The 727 banks.
Ginger ale & another pill.

Through the window, below,
the river not a river, a navy stocking
sloughed & tossed. In the dark,

a forest can be mistaken for a body

of water. (*Your mask before others'* . . .)

The captain has turned . . .
                    You may move freely . . .

Behind you, encorona, the sun,
& I in the grass, looking up, saw a plane
insectile (without my glasses)
fly through your head
in one ear & out the other.

An illusion. The first love poems I knew were

prayers. What then of free fall's
rash grace, wings sheared & released
into other trajectories? (Daedalus winds
the alleys, gathered as wreckage
in the arms of a harlot.)

It's been so long since: the river

not a river through the thick
glass. A name.
                    Tennessee, Liffey,
Lethe. I hold my cup of ice against

my neck, the stranger's hand

next to me grazed
in the turbulence quaking.

Bertillonage Fragment, IV:
Oreille droite

if it is not
a parable it must be told like one

a man deaf in one ear hears
only one side

of a story unless he turns
around a parable is an instruction

with different facial hair a tree
is the same tree

regardless of the fullness
or color of the leaves many new

officers believe
when first hired every man

who says he's innocent
if one listens to birds

all his life he will not hear them
anymore one day

their calls are fire
signals between sentry towers their wings fluttering

are forged papers we reach
a verdict—

all innocent & guilty just the same.

Latent Print: Pale Suits

Cuffs rolled to the elbow & beneath
the white linen, a collarless tee, Miami

pink. My father's friends, '86
chic in tweed loafers, combed Sellecks

or a fine stubble. Slung low on the belt
the badge & gun stuffed in the waist, off-

duty, lost down the leg,   *Thud,*—
& the restaurant chokes on *amour-propre*

so bow & pick up your weapon. Flash
your gilted hip, servant. As you straighten,

they'll turn back to their meals & forgive
you. Someone will think, *If Christ came back*

today he'd wear white   linen with soft
lapels,   & you fall in love with the calm

voices laced with static on the dispatch
& when waking to the blue flickering

light, you can't know if it's the television
or a joyride in a squad car or the hottest

part of the flame. No one is safe. My father's
friends steal toilets off the lawns of domestics—

& leave them in each others' yards, full
of hot pink petunias. *They're real cards,*

they're animals. They eat greasy at Nikki's
on Cherokee Blvd. They grab the night

by the collar. *Anything you say can & will*
be used against you—   I've forgotten.

I speak.   If we don't believe
in these things, they are not true. The handcuffs

fall like silver ribbons   , the black
uniform rips on a nail. Bow & pick up

your weapon. Now   anything blunt will do.

Mourner with Cowl, Hands in His Sleeves

The docent says I can't have a pen
in this room, I can't write
with a pen—   *No ink, ink stains*—

only the erasable, only

the easily removed, and if I were
to use a pencil to vandalize
with mustache or initials
one of the thirty-seven Mourners

of Dijon, it would be her job
(*and pleasure*)
to have me thrown out

in handcuffs. A friend says: *Never*

trust an establishment
that doesn't have graffiti in the bathroom
stalls. It's a good thing

she's here, the docent warns,
It's a good thing:

my purse is almost big
enough to slip in one
of the statuettes like a small chic
dog, and walk out.

Last week, a woman was carrying

such a huge *pocketbook*
that when turning to walk
away from a Monet, the bag scraped
the canvas. I say,

that must have made you

very nervous,   tucking
my hands into my pockets, a sign

of fidelity, and turn

to walk the display of alabaster
bishops, monks, choirboys, a foot
and a half high each, egg white

in color except for their rosaries,
books, the aspergillum, all the color
of smudged away

lipstick. They once processed,
or seemed to, a kind of danse macabre, at the base
of the tombs of the Dukes
of Burgundy, until ravaged by revolution,

sold off, stolen, or destroyed, most

kept in private collections
as spoil, as totem to a lost kingdom—

The docent says there's a film
playing in the next room, perhaps I'd like to see

the Mourners in context
of the interviewed historians?
I've stopped watching

television news. The last
postcard my father sent—the ruins
of Shahr-e-Gholghola, *the City of*

Screams,

a ghost town of Genghis Kahn,
pillaged in the Afghan Civil War. I know my father

never left Bagram to see the site
dissolving into the desert, like hourglass
pillars, the postcard sold
at the Exchange

and written at his office desk, in the lab
with its vials, its radial

maps of bomb blasts, blood splatter, or else

the contractor's quarters. *There are others*
that are lost, you know,
the docent says,   *ones they never*

found. By now, others have
arrived in the gallery, a boy in uniform
reaches out to touch *Mourner*

with Cowl, Hands in His

Sleeves. The docent roars, alive
in her watchfulness—
I never wrote back, never

sent what I'd written,

for the father I've looted,
the ruined city
I could reach out to but never touch.

Notes

"Subject in the Position of the Soldier with No Arms" takes its title from a plate in Alphonse Bertillon's *Signaletic Instructions including the theory and practice of Anthropometrical Identification* (1896).

"Vanitas (Latent Print)" is in memory of my brother Nicholas Phillips (2001–2012).

"Entra Tutto" relies on fragments of Shakespeare, Dante, and Lombroso for contextual layering, as well as the discussions found within Stephen Jay Gould's *Mismeasure of Man* (1981). The lyrics that appear in the second section are from the poem "Stonewall Jackson's Way" by John Williamson Palmer, later set to music.

"Latent Print" refers to the term for the chance recording of fingerprint; the photograph referenced is *Thomas Eakins Carrying a Woman* (1885).

In "Triptych: Automata, " Descartes's "Francine" is the only one whose existence has never been verified. "Tipu's Tiger" is on display at the Victoria & Albert Museum and "The Flute Player" was documented but did not survive.

The "Bertillonage Fragments" found throughout the collection are loosely based on measurements described in Bertillon's *Signaletic Instructions including the theory and practice of Anthropometrical Identification* (1896).

"Blues Dream" is for Jeremy.

"Diaspora" is for Gregory Kimbrell.

"Cross Section" references the elephant clock described in of Al-Jazari's medieval *Book of the Knowledge of Ingenious Mechanical Devices* (1206).

"Sublimation" uses selections from the twelfth-century alchemy text "The Turba Philosophorum" and *The Works of Ossian* (1765), a hoaxed Scots epic written by its "translator" James MacPherson. The final lines of this poem are Morse code.

"The Speech of Monkeys" takes its title from the title from R. L. Garner's book of the same name (1892).

"Post" borrows imagery from the story of the bee in the Qur'an, specifically 16:69: "Then eat from all the fruits and follow the ways of your Lord laid down [for you]. There emerges from their bellies a drink, varying in colors, in which there is healing for people. Indeed in that is a sign for a people who give thought."

"The Ear: General Form & Separation of the Internal Windings" takes its title from a plate in Alphonse Bertillon's *Signaletic Instructions including the theory and practice of Anthropometrical Identification* (1896).

"Cuspis" is for Jeremy. Dental technicians use soap to practice making false teeth for crowns, bridges, and dentures.

"Ars Poetica (Latent Print)" borrows a line from Jeremy Bentham's *Panopticon Writings*.

"Skin Mags" borrows a line from Milton's *Paradise Lost*. This poem is for Tracy.

"Niedecker's Iron" is after Lorine Niedecker's letters to Louis Zukofsky and his son, Paul, and her sequence, "For Paul."

"Reading Joyce on US Flight 2309" makes specific references to *Portrait of the Artist as a Young Man* (1916).

"Mourner with Cowl, Hands in His Sleeves" refers to the Mourners who were positioned at the base of the tombs of Philip the Bold and John the Fearless, the Dukes of Burgundy.

Acknowledgments

Many thanks to those publications in which these poems previously appeared, sometimes with different titles and in varied forms: *AGNI*: "*Entra Tutto*"; *Asheville Poetry Review*: "Vanitas (Latent Print)"; *Beloit Poetry Journal*: "Cross Section," "Niedecker's Iron"; *Cerise Press*: "Diaspora," "Mourner with Cowl, Hands in His Sleeves"; *Connotations Press: An Online Artifact*: "Latent Print," "Reading Joyce on U.S. Flight 2309," "The Ear: General Form & Separation of the Internal Windings"; *Copper Nickel*: "Blues Dream," "The Speech of Monkeys"; *diode*: "Bertillonage Fragment, II: *Buste*," "Bertillonage Fragment, III: *Longueur de la tête & Largeur de la tête*," "Post," "Triptych: Automata" (originally published as "Triptych: Automata, I," "Triptych: Automata, III,"); *Ecotone*: "Skin Mags"; *Green Mountains Review*: "Latent Print: Indicia," "Latent Print: Interrogation Helix,"; *Gulf Coast*: "Latent Print: Pale Suits"; *Hayden's Ferry Review*: "The Study Heads"; *Indiana Review*: "Bertillonage Fragment, IV: *Oreille droite*"; *The Journal*: "*In vacuo*, Universal Studios"; *The Kenyon Review*: "Sublimation"; *Poems & Plays*: "Ghost Sonnet"; *Superstition Review*: "Bertillonage Fragment, I: *Taille*"; *Sycamore Review*: "Ars Poetica (Latent Print)," "Subject in the Position of the Soldier with No Arms"; *Third Coast*: "Teratoma." "Cuspis" appeared in the chapbook, *Strange Meeting* (Eureka Press, 2010).

Many thanks to Zoland Poetry for reprinting "Subject in the Position of the Soldier with No Arms," "Cuspis," "Latent Print," "Blues Dream," "Ghost Sonnet," "Skin Mags," and "Ars Poetica (Latent Print)" as a feature on their website. Much gratitude to *The Journal* and judge G.C. Waldrep for naming "*In vacuo*, Universal Studios" the winner of the 2012 Poetry Contest; *Cutthroat: A Journal of the Arts* for naming "Subject in the Position of the Soldier with No Arms" a finalist in the 2010 Joy Harjo Poetry Prize; *Copper Nickel* for naming "Blues Dream" a finalist in their 2011 Poetry Prize; and *Sycamore Review* for naming "Ars Poetica (Latent Print)" a finalist for the 2011 Wabash Poetry Prize.

I would like to thank my teachers Tom Balázs, Earl Braggs, Greg Donovan, Kathy Graber, Rick Jackson, and especially David Wojahn for giving me a headlamp at the mouth of the tunnel; Mark Cox, Denise Dicks, Thom Didato, Caitlin Doyle, Claudia Emerson, Joshua Gottlieb-Miller, Creech Hardee, Gregory Kimbrell, Joey Kingsley, Martha Mabry, Sebastian Matthews, Nick McRae, Lena Moses-Schmitt, Georgia Sams, Seth Sams, Tom Sleigh, Bri Spicer, Tracy Tanner, and Patrick Scott Vickers for the chorus of *Polo*s to my wee *Marco*; the Sewanee Writers' Conference; Vermont Studio Center and Zoland Poetry for allowing me the space and time to revise the manuscript; all the MFA students at Virginia Commonwealth University; editors and staff of *Blackbird* as yet unnamed especially Mary Flinn, Michael Keller, Randy Marshall, and Susan Settlemyre Williams; Mary Biddinger and the University of Akron Press for their confidence in the book; my friends; my family, especially my mother, my father, my grandparents, and Sonia; the Hakes and Lewis families; and Jeremy, bis and forte.